REMOVE THE LEAD FROM **LEAD**ER**SHIP** BEFORE YOUR SHIP SINKS

Empowering Today's Youth to Become Powerful
and Outstanding Leaders God's Way!

Leadership Book & Study Guideto Staying Anchored

Skills To Stay Afloat
Carolyn J. Kirk

When the righteous are in authority the people rejoice… Proverbs 29:2. [KJV]

WESTBOW
P R E S S®
A DIVISION OF THOMAS NELSON
& ZONDERVAN

Interior Image Credit: Carolyn J. Kirk, Author, Motivational Speaker and Life Coach.

WestBow Press books may be ordered through booksellers or by contacting:

WestBow Press
A Division of Thomas Nelson & Zondervan
1663 Liberty Drive
Bloomington, IN 47403
www.westbowpress.com
1 (866) 928-1240

ISBN: 978-1-9736-2737-1 (sc)
ISBN: 978-1-9736-2738-8 (e)

Library of Congress Control Number: 2018905388

Print information available on the last page.

WestBow Press rev. date: 05/07/2018

Table of Contents

When the righteous are in authority the people rejoice. Proverbs 29:2. (KJV)

Book Dedication:

This book is dedicated to two women I most admired,
Pearlie Mae Lobley-Davis & Shirley Ann Davis-Cross.
Ongoing examples of unconditional love.
Encouragers, whose words and examples were so heart
felt and inspirational, impacted me for a life-time.
My heart is warmed from thoughts of them daily.
My Mother & My sister,
Pearlie Mae Lobley-Davis, my mother,
& Shirley Ann Davis-Cross, my sister.

Acknowledgment
Erica and Carly!

I want to give honor to my Lord and Savior, Jesus Christ who is the head of my life. Thank you, Lord, for making it possible for me to write this book. To my beautiful daughters, Erica and Carly, I want to express my gratitude to you both for believing and supporting me while writing this book. You are truly my heroes and a blessing from God. You are strong and precious young women, beautiful inside and out. I love you and appreciate you so much. You are exemplary examples of God-fearing women, demonstrated by your unwavering love for Christ. You are testimonies of how young women should live "on purpose," for God. Thank you for letting me mother you, help you, lead you, and love you God's way.

A shout out to Sharon, Ernestine, Erica, Diane, Carly, Lisa and Melinda for helping me in the process of editing and proofreading. Thanks for allowing me to talk things over, help with reorganization, offering suggestions, comments, and allowing me to use a quote (Sharon).

I also wish to thank the rest of my family, who provided support and encouraged me to take this journey.

To God be the glory!

Purpose of my book:

The purpose of this Leadership Book and Study Guide is to share my desire and passion to see the next youth of our generation strive as great leaders in an era of anger, rage and disobedience. I see so many youths today that are so angry and upset about everything; yet, not able to deal with their life circumstances. This book and guide will equip our youth in dealing with weights that once were too heavy to bear.

1

The Start of Leadership

From the beginning of time, the two most important leadership qualities have been 1.) Authority, and 2.) Influence. God created the first man, Adam, and then created the first woman, Eve. God put Adam and Eve in the Garden of Eden to care and nurture the land. He told Adam and Eve that they could eat from any fruit of the trees except for the tree of good and evil. God warned them that if they ate from this tree they would die.

One day Satan came disguised as a snake and spoke to Eve, convincing her to eat the fruit from the tree of good and evil. Eve told the serpent that God said they should not eat it and they would die if they did; however, Satan tempted Eve to eat saying that she would become like God if she did. Eve believed the lie and took a bite of the fruit. She then gave some to Adam for him to eat. Adam and Eve, now knowing that they had sinned, immediately felt ashamed and tried to hide from God.

God gave Adam authority (leader) and Eve follower) influence. When things get out of order the wrong people take the lead and things are never the same.

2

There is Safety in the Boat

Therefore, since we are surrounded by so great a cloud of witnesses [who have borne testimony to the Truth], let us strip off and throw aside every encumbrance (unnecessary weight) and that sin which so readily (deftly and cleverly) clings to and entangles us, and let us run with patient endurance and steady and active persistence the appointed course of the race that is set before us,... Hebrews 12:1 (AMPC)

The bible is referring to a spiritual confidence: knowing in your heart who God is, who he can be in your life, and what he can do in and through you. We can be assured and have confidence that we will not sink under the pressures and the weights of life and sail into the comfort of our heavenly father's purpose. God is our heavenly father, and He loves us and cares for us and wants the best for us. The thing that we need to keep in mind is that we are his children and he will never forsake us. There is nothing more that we can do to earn God's approval. We are safe in his arms. There is safety in the boat, just as Peter stepped out in faith, we can weather the storms of life when we learn to remove the lead (weights) from our lives. Use your boat for your platform to success.

Please relax and enjoy this book. I pray that you will be inspired to lead, learn and live to the glory of God.

Minding the ship to avoid a mental wreck!

Included in this chapter is a listing of words and definitions having to do with ships and sailing, from A to Z. These terms come mainly from the 16th to 18th centuries, which is also known as the great age of sailing ships. The purpose of this exercise is to keep you mindful of the attitude you need to have to avoid sinking. It has everything to do with our thinking…

Finally, brothers, whatever is true, whatever is noble, whatever is right, whatever is pure, whatever is lovely, whatever is admirable—if anything is excellent or praiseworthy—think about such things. Whatever you have learned or received or heard from me or seen in me—put it into practice. And the God of peace will be with you. Philippians 4:8,9 KJV

We are to spend our time thinking about the things that are accurate, genuine, and reliable. To do this, we need to do at least three things.

First, we must become aware of the falsehoods that masquerade as truth.

We must learn to think consciously. Will you make a conscious choice to think positive today?

Second, we must be intentional about pursuing the truth.

Make time to read and interact with the bible daily.

We must tell ourselves the truth.

Would you call that a positive or a negative comment?

How do you think God would view this situation?

I hope you get the idea of," minding the ship to avoid a mental wreck". The task may be annoying at first (and maybe a little challenging), but I know you will appreciate the outcome.

No one wants to be a negative thinker. We want to be godly thinkers. I pray that you walk in the sweetness of God's peace. So, I pray this will encourage you to think better thoughts. We all may grumble at the time . . .but we become grateful . . . eventually.

Ship Terms and Definitions

*Derived from: Nautical Terms. (n.d.). Retrieved from http://phrontistery. info/nautical.html

Ship Terms	Ship Definitions	Relate the ship terms and definitions to the mind of a leader. Be creative!
A-Aboard	on or within the boat	
B-boatswain	ship's crewmember in charge of equipment and maintenance	
C-cast off	to let go.	
D- Dead ahead	directly ahead.	
E- EBB	a receding current.	
F- flood	a incoming current.	
G- gybe	to swing a sail from one side to another	
H- helm	ship's steering wheel	
I- inboard	inside the line of a ship's bulwarks or hull	

J- jibe	to change a ship's course to make the boom shift sides	
K- kedge	small anchor to keep a ship steady	
L- larboard	left side of a ship	
M- moonraker	topmost sail of a ship, above the skyscraper	
N-navigation	the art and science of conducting a boat safely from one point to another	
O- overboard	over the side or out of the boat	
P- pallograph	instrument measuring ship's vibration	
Q- quartering	sailing nearly before the wind	
R- reef	to reduce area of a sail by rolling or folding part of it	
S- supercargo	ship's official in charge of business affairs	
T- tranship	to transfer from one ship to another	
U- unreeve	to withdraw a rope from an opening	
V-V bottom	a hull with the bottom section in the shape of a "V"	
W- watching	fully afloat	
X- xebec	small three-masted pirate ship	
Y- yawl	ship's small boat; sailboat carrying mainsail and one or more jibs	
Z- zabra	small Spanish sailing vessel	

3

Cast Negative Thoughts Overboard

"Cast all your anxiety on him because he cares for you." 1 Peter 5:7- NIV

One of the fastest ways of sinking is to think negatively. The bible makes it very clear, *"For as he thinketh in his heart, so is he:" Proverbs 23:7, (KJV).* According to the book of Jonah 11:12 (KJV), when Jonah was asked what needed to be done to stop the storm, he said they had to throw him overboard into the sea. Why did he put the responsibility on them, the crew, and not just say I am the one. He simply could have said I need to jump overboard to end the storm? Instead he seems to put the burden on the crew rather than take care of the solution himself. Just poor judgement, on Jonah's part.

The story of the prodigal son begins with a man who has two sons. The younger son asks his father for his portion of the family estate as an early inheritance. Once received, the son promptly sets off on a long journey to a distant land and begins to waste his fortune on wild living.

When the money runs out, a severe famine hits the country and the son finds himself in dire circumstances. He takes a job feeding pigs. Eventually, he grows so destitute that he even longs to eat the food assigned to the pigs.

The young man finally comes to his senses (right thinking) and remembers his father. In humility, the son recognizes his foolishness and decides to return to his father and ask for forgiveness and mercy. The father who has been watching and waiting, receives his son back with open arms of compassion. He is overjoyed by the return of his lost son. [Luke 15:11(KJV)]

Once we come to our senses, our heavenly father is watching and waiting to receive us back to him.

Speak to the storm to calm the sea!

As leaders we have authority. The devil wants you to think it would be crazy to talk to things. But it's not. God word says..." *He replied, "Because you have so little faith. Truly I tell you, if you have faith as small as a mustard seed, you can say to this mountain, 'Move from here to there,' and it will move. Nothing will be impossible for you." [Luke 17:6 NLT]*

The bible is a message from God. It gives us instruction for our benefit and practical advice for everyday living. It's time to take the bible down off the pedestal, read it, and act on its instructions. Too many people think of the bible only as a holy book to be revered. So they put it up on a shelf, dust it off every now and then, and make sure no one mistreats it.

Jesus spoke everything into existence. He spoke to sickness. He spoke to the storm and told it to be still. He spoke to dead bodies and commanded them to get up. He spoke to trees. And he spoke to the devil and told him to get behind him. Jesus spoke to things. We should too. You should speak to fear and worry. You should speak to confusion. You should speak to lack. You should speak to sickness. You should speak to the devil. Tell them to leave. Tell them to "be removed." SAY THIS: Jesus said I can speak to things. So, I speak to everything that is of the devil and command it to get out of my life now! Remember, as the leaders, we have been given authority to speak to things.

What are Leadership Skills?

Leadership skills can be learned and developed by anyone. They include all the qualities necessary to guide a group from one point to another. Leaders use their personal knowledge, skills and influence to establish relationships with people and help others meet their goals.

Leaders need to understand varieties of leadership styles, skills and qualities and know in which situations to use them. Ideal leaders can lead and teach leadership at the same time. They share their talents with group members so that everyone may benefit and grow. Leader's become effective by modeling the skills and characteristics they seek to pass on to others. They acquire trust by being a person of good character and they achieve power by empowering others.

Leadership is something you believe in, but also something you put into action!

A great way to learn about leadership is through developing leadership skills.

How to Achieve Your Leadership Objectives

Learning how to achieve your goals and objectives is the key to reaching your life long dreams. While hope can provide the energy and the desire to reach you goals, it takes careful planning to achieve your goals. If you find yourself making little to no progress in achieving your goals, the following formula will help.

1. *Be specific on what you want.*

How will you accomplish the following?

• Achieve a clear understanding of the meaning of leadership and the qualities of a leader.

How:_____

_____

_____

• Acquire leadership skills and understanding of working with others.

How:_____

_____

_____

• Participate in team building.

How:_____

_____

_____

• Develop follow-through and responsibility.

How:_____

_____

_____

- Improve written, verbal and interpersonal communication skills.

How:_____

_____

_____

- Gain self-confidence and self-respect.

How:_____

_____

_____

- Practice and acquire leadership skills.

How:_____

_____

_____

2. *Cast it over board*. Once you have developed a new plan, let go of the anchor (sink the past). Set afloat all your past failures and accomplishments, you are done with them! It is a new adventure for you now and the message is full speed ahead. Committing yourself emotionally to the next steps is easier said than done. This may require a level of self-discipline you are not comfortable with. However, attaining your goals is well worth the effort.

What are some things you need to cast overboard in taking the next step toward your new goal(s) and objective(s)?

_____

_____

_____

_____

_____

_____
_____
_____
_____
_____

3. _**Shout it out**_. There's nothing like telling others about your goals to hold you accountable. Tell somebody, tell your family, tell your co-workers, tell your church family, and tell your neighbors. The more people you have, the more advocates you will have. These advocates will also help to keep you honest should you falter.

What's your main three goals as a leader?

Goal (s):

1. _____
   _____
2. _____
   _____
3. _____
   _____

4. _**Write it all down (Journaling)**_. Keep a journal of leadership skills you've learned and practiced as a leader in the categories listed below. Writing something down is a simple yet powerful tool to help visualize the achievement of establishing your objectives and reaching your goals. Write down your goals with all the details as many details as possible.

- Communicating:

Goal:

_____

_____

- Decision- making and problem solving:

Goal:

_____

_____

- Resolving conflicts (negotiating):

Goal:

_____

_____

- Motivating people:

Goal:

_____

_____

- Creating positive feedback:

Goal:

_____

_____

- Gaining self-confidence:

Goal:

_____

_____

- Delegating tasks:

Goal:

_____

_____

5. _Rejoice._ Don't forget to reward yourself for achieving milestones. Whether your goal is big or small, have a celebration and tell the world! This will affirm your objectives and help to build a ritual around success. It will also help you to recommit yourself to achieving your ultimate objectives.

What is your ultimate objective(s)?

Objective(s):

_____

_____

_____

_____

4

Leadership Life Skills from A to Z

Write skills (acronyms) for each of these floaters:

A – Attitude

"Life is a shipwreck, but we must not forget to sing in the lifeboats. ~Voltaire"

Definition: An attitude is an expression of favor or disfavor toward a person, place, thing, or event (the attitude object). Attitude can be formed from a person's past and present.

A	
T	
T	
I	
T	
U	
D	
E	

B – Boundaries

"When you say "Yes" to others…make sure you are not saying "No" to yourself." Paulo Coelho.

Definition: Boundaries are guidelines, rules or limits that a person creates to identify reasonable, safe and permissible ways for other people to behave towards them and how they will respond when someone passes those limits. They are built out of a mix of conclusions, beliefs, opinions, attitudes, past experiences and social learning.

B	
O	
U	
N	
D	
A	
R	
I	
E	
S	

C –Communication

"Communication is the real work of leadership". Nitin Nohria

Definition: The successful conveying or sharing of ideas and feelings. Communication is the act of conveying intended meaning to another entity through the use of mutually understood signs and rules. The basic steps of communication are the forming of communicative intent, message composition, message encoding, transmission of signal, reception of signal, message decoding and finally interpretation of the message by the recipient.

C	
O	
M	
M	
U	
N	
I	
C	
A	
T	
I	
O	
N	

D – Delegate

"Delegating work works, provided the one delegating works, too." -Robert Half

Definition: A person sent or authorized to represent others.

D	
E	
L	
E	
G	
A	
T	
E	

E – Effort

"Your results will reflect your efforts." Sharon Phillips

Definition: Effort is defined as the use of physical or mental energy, the act or result of trying to do something. An example of effort is someone using his or her brain to plan. An example of effort is writing a letter.

E	
F	
F	
O	
R	
T	

F – Flexibility

"I think there is a big and significant difference between being a leader and being a manager-leaders lead from the heart. You have to be analytical and flexible. Flexibility is one of the key ingredients to being successful. If you feel like it's difficult to change, you will probably have a harder time succeeding." — Andrea Jung

Definition: Flexibility is defined as the ability to change, to bend, or to persuade. An example of flexibility is being able to work whenever one wants.

F	
L	
E	
X	
I	

B	
I	
L	
I	
T	
Y	

G – Goals

"Without goals, and plans to reach them, you are like a ship that has set sail with no destination." Fitzhugh Dodson

Definition: Goals: The end toward which effort is directed.

G	
O	
A	
L	
S	

H – Honesty

"Let us raise a standard to which the wise and honest can repair; the rest is in the hands of God." George Washington

Definition: The quality or fact of being honest; uprightness and fairness.

H	
O	
N	
E	
S	

T	
Y	

I – Integrity

"Have the courage to say no. Have the courage to face the truth. Do the right thing because it is right. These are the magic keys to living your life with integrity." W. Clement Stone

Definition: The quality of being honest and having strong moral principles; moral uprightness.

I	
N	
T	
E	
G	
R	
I	
T	
Y	

J- Justice

"If you spend your time hoping someone will suffer the consequences for what they did to your heart, then you're allowing them to hurt you a second time in your mind." — Shannon L. Alder

Definition: Just behavior or treatment: "A concern for justice, peace, and genuine respect for people. The quality of being fair and reasonable:

J	

U	
S	
T	
I	
C	
E	

K – Key Results

"The Six Steps to Success: 1) Define Success, 2) Devise a Plan, 3) Execute and Overcome Adversity, 4) Measure Results with Key Metrics, 5) Revise the Plan, and 6) Work Hard". — Ken Poirot

Definition: Key Result Area in this phrase key means a vital, crucial element. Key Result area refers to general areas of outputs or outcomes for which the department's role is responsible.

Your Key Result Areas are those things that you absolutely, positively must do to fulfill your responsibilities and achieve your goals.

K	
E	
Y	
R	
E	
S	
U	
L	
T	
S	

L – Leadership

"The mediocre teacher tells. The good teacher explains. The superior teacher demonstrates. The great teacher inspires." — William Arthur Ward

Definition: The action of leading a group of people or an organization.

L	
E	
A	
D	
E	
R	
S	
H	
I	
P	

M – Motivation

"Problems are not stops signs, they are guidelines." Robert H. Schuller

Definition: The act or process of giving someone a reason for doing something: the act or process of motivating someone. The condition of being eager to act or work: the condition of being motivated.

M	
O	
T	
I	
V	
A	

T	
I	
O	
N	

N – Negotiation

"Negotiation is not a policy. It's a technique. It's something you use when it's to your advantage, and something that you don't use when it's not to your advantage. "John Bolton

Definition: The process of discussing something with someone in order to reach an agreement, or the discussions themselves

N	
E	
G	
O	
T	
I	
A	
T	
I	
O	
N	

O – Objectives

"Leadership is working with goals and vision; management is working with objectives. "Russel Honore

Definition: Something that one's efforts or actions are intended to attain or accomplish; purpose; goal; target.

O	
B	
J	
E	
C	
T	
I	
V	
E	
S	

P– Purpose

"Believe in your heart that you're meant to live a life full of passion, purpose, magic and miracles." — Roy T. Bennett

Definition: The reason for which something is done or created or for which something exists.

P	
U	
R	
P	
O	
S	
E	

Q – Quality

"Quality means doing it right when no one is looking." Henry Ford

"Quality is never an accident; it is always the result of high intention, sincere effort, intelligent direction and skillful execution; it represents the wise choice of many alternatives. Quality questions create a quality life." William A. Foster

Definition: The degree to which something meets or exceeds the expectations of its' consumers.

Q	
U	
A	
L	
I	
T	
Y	

R- Respect

"Respect for ourselves guides our morals, respect for others guides our manners." Laurence Sterne

R	
E	
S	
P	
E	
C	
T	

S – Self-esteem

"Wanting to be someone else is a waste of the person you are." — *Marilyn Monroe*

Definition: a feeling of pride in yourself.

S	
E	
L	
F	
E	
S	
T	
E	
E	
M	

T – Teamwork

"Teamwork is the ability to work together toward a common vision. The ability to direct individual accomplishments toward organizational objectives. It is the fuel that allows common people to attain uncommon results." —*Andrew Carnegie*

Definition: Cooperative or coordinated effort on the part of a group of persons acting together as a team or in the interests of a common cause.

T	
E	
A	
M	

W	
O	
R	
K	

U – Urgency

"Time to improve is limited. The clock is always on and doesn't care if you don't feel like it. Someone else does and they're passing you by."
— William James Moore,

definition: Importance requiring swift action.

U	
R	
G	
E	
N	
C	
Y	

V – Vision

"The most pathetic person in the world is someone who has sight but no vision."
— Helen Keller

Definition: An experience in which a person, thing, or event appears vividly or credibly to the mind, although not actually present, often under the influence of a divine or other agency.

V	
I	
S	
I	
O	
N	

W – Work Ethic

"You have to have a work ethic, and you have to be educated in what you're doing. You have to take it seriously. It doesn't mean that everything you do has to be serious. But you've got to have the tools." Jakob Dylan

Definition: A belief in the moral benefit and importance of work and its' inherent ability to strengthen character.

W	
O	
R	
K	
E	
T	
H	
I	
C	

X – Excellent

"Everybody is standing, but you must stand out. Everybody is breaking grounds; but you must breakthrough! Everybody is scratching it; but you must scratch it hard! Everybody is going, but you must keep

going extra miles! Dare to be exceptionally excellent and why not?"
— Israelmore Ayivor

Definition: Extremely good; outstanding.

E	
X	
C	
E	
L	
L	
E	
N	
T	

Y – You

"You were born with potential. You were born with goodness and trust. You were born with ideals and dreams. You were born with greatness. You were born with wings. You are not meant for crawling, so don't. You have wings. Learn to use them and fly." — Jalaluddin Mevlana Rumi

Definition: You.

Y	
O	
U	

Z – Zealous

"Perfection is pure action that comes with zeal to excel." — Vikrmn, Corpkshetra

Definition: Having or showing zeal. 'the council was extremely zealous in the application of the regulations'

Z	
E	
A	
L	
O	
U	
S	

5

"7 Effective Ways to Lead"

1. **Do it first. Be the example.**

   I worked for over 20 years in various industries as a Production Manager and Shift Supervisor. To get the desired results, I would perform the task first. Therefore, demonstrating the ability to obtain my desired outcome with a sense of urgency, quality and excellence.

2. **Express sincere gratitude to those willing to follow.**

   Gratitude is a great character trait to have. We all want to be acknowledgde for what we do. When kindness is genuine, it makes us willing to continue to follow.

3. **Listening to other's ideas.**

   One of the best skills to possess is listening to others. Always having the last word doesn't mean other ideas don't mean anything.

4. **Talk more about others ideas than about yours.**

   Brag about someone else. If you must always promote yourself, what is the point?

5. **Be authentically interested.**

   Don't fake it. If it not the most reasonable decision for the team, stay with the task until you achieve a common goal.

6. **Praise.**

   Specifically identify the area in which you are giving praise and admiration.

7. **Show appreciation.**

   Say thank you. Show your appreciation for their hard work and contributions. And, don't forget to say "please" often as well.

6

Top Leadership Verses in the Bible

Explain your thoughts regarding the verses below.

"Do nothing from selfishness or empty conceit, but with humility of mind regard one another as more important than yourselves." Philippians 2:3, NASB

Explain:

_____

_____

_____

"Treat others the same way you want them to treat you." Luke 6:31, NASB

Explain:

_____

_____

_____

"It is not this way among you, but whoever wishes to become great among you shall be your servant". Matthew 20:26, NASB

Explain:

_____

_____

_____

"He must increase, but I must decrease." John 3:30, NASB

Explain:

_____

_____

_____

"Where there is no guidance the people fall, but in abundance of counselors there is victory." Proverbs 11:14, NASB

Explain:

_____

_____

_____

"It is an abomination for kings to commit wicked acts, for a throne is established on righteousness." Proverbs 16:12, NASB

Explain:

_____

_____

_____

"So he shepherded them according to the integrity of his heart, And guided them with his skillful hands." Psalm 78:72, NASB

Explain:

_____

_____

_____

"Blessed are you, O land, whose king is of nobility and whose princes eat at the appropriate time--for strength and not for drunkenness." Ecclesiastes 10:17, NASB

Explain:

_____

_____

_____

"When the righteous increase, the people rejoice, but when a wicked man rules, people groan." Proverbs 29:2, NASB

Explain:

_____

_____

_____

"Furthermore, you shall select out of all the people able men who fear God, men of truth, those who hate dishonest gain; and you shall place these over them as leaders of thousands, of hundreds, of fifties and of tens." Exodus 18:21, NASB

Explain:

_____

_____

_____

"Be diligent to present yourself approved to God as a workman who does not need to be ashamed, accurately handling the word of truth." 2 Timothy 2:15, NASB

Explain:

_____

_____

_____

"But it is not this way with you, but the one who is the greatest among you must become like the youngest, and the leader like the servant." Luke 22:26, NASB

Explain:

_____

_____

_____

"If a king judges the poor with truth, His throne will be established forever". Proverbs 29:14, NASB

Explain:

_____

_____

_____

"The king gives stability to the land by justice, but a man who takes bribes overthrows it." Proverbs 29:4, NASB

Explain:

_____

_____

_____

"Watch over your heart with all diligence, for from it flows the springs of life." Proverbs 4:23, NASB

Explain:

_____

_____

_____

"Let us not lose heart in doing good, for in due time we will reap if we do not grow weary." Galatians 6:9, NASB

Explain:

_____

_____

_____

"Obey your leaders and submit to them, for they keep watch over your souls as those who will give an account. Let them do this with joy and not with grief, for this would be unprofitable for you." Hebrews 13:17, NASB

Explain:

_____

_____

_____

"(but if a man does not know how to manage his own household, how will he take care of the church of God?)," 1 Timothy 3:5, NASB

Explain:

_____

_____

_____

"For even as the body is one and yet has many members, and all the members of the body, though they are many, are one body, so also is Christ. For by one Spirit we were all baptized into one body, whether Jews or Greeks, whether slaves or free, and we were all made to drink of one Spirit. For the body is not one member, but many." 1 Corinthians 12:12-31, NASB

Explain:

_____

_____

_____

"For through the grace given to me I say to everyone among you not to think more highly of himself than he ought to think; but to think so as to have sound judgment, as God has allotted to each a measure of faith. For just as we have many members in one body and all the members do *not have the same function, so we, who are many, are one body in Christ, and individually members one of another." Romans 12:3-8, NASB*

Explain:

_____

_____

_____

"Holding to a form of godliness, although they have denied its power; Avoid such men as these." 2 Timothy 3:5, NASB

Explain:

_____

_____

_____

Footnote: Verses New American Standard Bible (NASB)

7

Youth Leadership Questionnaire:

1. Have you ever worked as a youth leader?

a. Yes. Once
b. Twice
c. No

2. Do you think youth leadership plays an essential role for the youth development?

a. Yes
b. No
c. Not sure

3. Have you ever attended any seminar on youth empowerment and youth leadership?

a. Once
b. Twice
c. Never attended
d. Others, please specify:

4. As a youth leader, are you aware about the youth needs?

a. Yes. I am aware
b. Not aware
c. Other remarks:

5. Choose the most effective leadership skill out of the followings of a youth leader.

a. Strong communication skills
b. Enthusiastic and strong determination
c. Sound knowledge of delegation
d. Good decision-making skills and problem-solving approach
e. All the above

6. What is the major role of a youth leader?

a. Measuring the needs and requirements of the youth group.
b. Fulfilling responsibilities to build morale.
c. Setting a clear vision, and leading others through the process.
d. Leading people toward the desired end by achieving goals.
e. All the above.

Youth Leadership Planning

I will be responsible for the following task:

_____

_____

I will work with (age and number of youth). My goal is to have a direct impact on:

_____

_____

How and when will I complete this task:

_____

_____

List of names of the people available to help, if needed:

_____

_____

List of specific skills and/or attitudes you plan to improve with your leadership plan:

_____

_____

Other preparation needed:

_____

_____

Youth Leader Signature of Commitment:

_____

8

Leadership Interest Survey

The youth leadership interest survey (self-assessment) aims at identifying leadership qualities in an individual. This survey is being used to ascertain the self-evaluation process of youth in leading others.

1. What is your comfort level while working with others?

a. Very comfortable
b. Comfortable
c. Average
d. Not at all

2. How good are your interpersonal skills?

a. Very good
b. Good
c. Need to improve
d. Poor

3. How good are you at making plans and empowering others to help you in implementing the same?

a. Very good
b. Good
c. Need some training in delegation
d. Not sure

4. Do you always pride yourself in abiding by all rules and regulations imposed on you?

a. Always
b. Most of the time
c. Very rarely
d. Never

5. Are you comfortable to go to others for counseling issues?

a. Yes
b. No
c. Depends

6. How would you rate your problem handling expertise?

a. Outstanding
b. Good
c. Average
d. Bad
e. Not sure

7. Have you always felt very comfortable to provide constructive feedback?

a. Very comfortable
b. Comfortable
c. Not comfortable
d. Depends

8. Do you know how to delegate work to others?

a. Yes
b. No
c. Maybe

9. How effective are you at handling complaints and resolving issues?

a. Very effective
b. Effective
c. Not effective
d. Not sure

10. Do you have what it takes to handle difficult tasks?

a. Yes
b. No
c. Not sure

11. Have you always been able to accept changes?

a. Yes
b. No
c. Not Sure

12. What would be the strongest quality you possess which would prove to be a good leader?

Answer:_____

Can you Identify?

Signs of A Bad Leader

It's an interesting challenge. Say you're a manager, or a human resources employee, your job is to be a leader. Yes, but your job is also to pick out leaders, to select who will be promoted, given extra responsibility, and head up a project or team. How do you know who will make a great leader in a given circumstance?

There are several trainings regarding different attributes that make great leaders great, but what makes a poor leader? We can all pick them out after the fact (hindsight is 20/20 after all).

The following traits would be a red flag that you might not be ready for a leadership position:

☐ Do you lack empathy? The lack of compassion is a key indicator of a poor leader. If the person cannot seem to put him or herself in another person's shoes and see things from a different perspective, they will never be a truly great leader.

☐ Do you fear change? Change is terrifying for everyone, especially when it involves relationships and/or people's jobs. But leaders who cannot embrace change are destined to be left behind.

☐ Are you too willing to compromise? The ability to find a win/win situation is a gift for a leader. However, anyone who is too quick to compromise his or her ideas are not going to be a benefit to the team. It's a fine balance between understanding when to give in and when to stand your ground.

☐ Are you a "Bossy Betty"? It's a common misconception that bossy people make good bosses. Actually, the opposite is true. Someone who simply orders others around is unlikely to stimulate any loyalty or make subordinates feel empowered.

☐ Are you too indecisive? Leaders must make decisions. If a person always seems to waver on choices, big and small, one example where should a certain client go for lunch. They may have difficulty in a leadership position. Indecisiveness indicates a lack of self-confidence.

☐ Are you a "know it all?" Sometimes we want to impress others by appearing that we have control of the situation and have all the answers. Accomplishing more alone does not show subordinates we are team players. It can also signal that the leader may have unreasonable expectations of the rest of the team.

☐ Do you have a poor judge of character? A person who is naive when it comes to friends and coworkers, making excuses or being unable to see another's true character, will not surround himself with the kinds of people who will help him rise to the top.

☐ Are you out of balance? Someone who is the first into the office every day and the last to leave might seem like a great candidate for promotion. But ask yourself if they have any balance in their lives. A lack of balance can be a precursor to burnout.

☐ Do you have a lack of humility? The person who acts as though they can do it all and are the only one who can do it right is unlikely to rise to be a great leader, because they'll be too busy doing everyone else's job.

☐ This is not to say that having one of these characteristics automatically bars anyone from assuming a leadership position. In fact, I believe people can learn to overcome any of these bad habits and become a better leader.

☐ If you exhibit more than one trait on this list, it's a good bet that you're not ready to lead currently. If you are willing to grow, give them the opportunity to improve. You'll be able to model how a great leader really works.

What characteristics do you think indicate someone is or will be a poor leader?

Comments:_____

_____

_____

_____

9

Level of Leadership Survey

How can you lead if you have weights holding you back? Take a moment and check your level of leadership:

Directions: Please circle the number for each question that best describes your agreement with each statement.

Questions	Strongly Agree	Agree Somewhat	Disagree Somewhat	Strongly Disagree
1. I feel that I'm a person of influence, at least on an equal par with others.	3	2	1	0
2. I feel that I am confident and can influence others.	3	2	1	0
3. All in all, I am inclined to feel that I'm a good person.	3	2	1	0
4. I can do things as well as most other people.	3	2	1	0
5. I feel I do not have much to be proud of because of my low self-esteem.	3	2	1	0
6. I take a positive attitude toward other.	3	2	1	0

7. Overall, I am satisfied with myself.	3	2	1	0
8. I have respect for those in authority.	3	2	1	0
9. I feel useless at times.	3	2	1	0
10. I know my purpose.	3	2	1	0
11. I have hope for my future.	3	2	1	0
12. I feel that people see my worth.	3	2	1	0
13. I am very judgmental.	3	2	1	0
14. I depend on others to make me happy.	3	2	1	0
15. I depend on others to validate me.	3	2	1	0

Scoring: Point values are as indicated above, to score the test, the point's values of each response should be summed. A higher score indicates greater leadership. Lower scores indicate areas for growth. The following exercises will aide you in identifying your level of confidences, self-esteem, respect, influence, and authority.

10

Confidence

One of the most important and necessary characteristic of a good leader is having confidence in who you are. Do you know someone who is very confident? I believe confident people are destined for greatness. We are always told to be self-confident. When we look up bible verses on self-confidence, we read mostly verses that explain how our confidence comes from God. It starts in the beginning with God creating the earth and designating humanity to watch over it. God shows over and over that he has confidence in us. As christians we are always told to avoid focusing too much on the self and to focus on God.

Confidence can be misleading. Feeling good about yourself is so easy to put at the will of others when it should only be up to you. The good news is that you're in control of how you choose to live your life. If you aren't as confident now as you like, just fake it till you make it…look the part. If you know that you look like a confident, and capable person, eventually you'll start to feel like one too.

How to fake it? Perfect your posture. How you conduct yourself communicates a lot to other people, so make sure you're telling them that you're confident and in-charge. Your posture is very important. Keep your shoulders back, your spine straight, and your chin high. Walk with purpose instead of dragging your feet and sit up straight. When you look like a confident person on the outside, you'll be approached as one by those around you.

So, what does the bible say about self-confidence? "I can do all this through him who gives me strength." Philippians 4:13. (NIV) "For the Lord will be your confidence and will keep your foot from being caught." Proverbs 3:26. (ESV) "Therefore, do not throw away your confidence, which has a great reward. For you have need of endurance, so that when you have done the will of God, you may receive what was promised." Hebrews 10:35-36. (NASB)

The more confident you are with the things of God, the more confident you will become in conquering the challenges this world may bring.

Acronym -Confidence

C	Be **_confident_** in who you are.
O	*Literally speaking... taking* **Ownership.**
N	**_Never_** give up.
F	**Fake** it till you make it.
I	Do not "only" allow others to **_influence_** you. Your purpose is to **_influence_** others (positively).
D	**Develop** your strengths.
E	Be **_Excellent_** ...to do good works.
N	**_"No"_** is no.
C	I **_can_** do all things (I can attitude).
E	Work on building a higher self-**_Esteem_**.

Who is the most confident person(s) you know?

_____

_____

_____

11

Self-Esteem

The purpose of this chapter is to help clarify and point you in the right direction in building a stronger foundation and level of self-esteem that supersedes even your greatest expectation.

Where do I start? As someone who grew up with four brothers, Jimmie Jr, (my twin brother), Gary, Randy and Anthony (twins), and eight sisters, Shirley, Diane, Delores, Cathy, Lisa, Jackie, Tammy and Gwen, "Pearl's Girls" you better know who you are and have some idea of your purpose. The definition of self-esteem according to Merriam-Webster- "confidence in one's own worth or abilities, self-respect". Someone with positive self-esteem will generally approach things head on, and think they are the right person for the task at hand. They are bold and courageous, they feel they deserve love and support, and believe they are destined to succeed in life.

On the other hand, someone with low or negative self-esteem will generally think they are not good at things, have no purpose and don't deserve love or support. Any situations that they face will work out badly for them.

As young girls my (8) eight sisters and I all have different levels of self-esteem, which is very normal for large family members. "Pearl's Girls" self-esteem levels (high) was evident by our positive image of ourselves and our self-confidence. We each made friends easily and are not anxious regarding new tasks, challenges or around new people. We try and solve problems on our own but are not ashamed to ask for help if needed.

When you walk in confidence and maintain high self-esteem you can be proud of your achievements. Because of the high self-esteem we can admit our shortcomings easier and remain teachable to learn from them. We are willing to try new things and adapt to change. As you can imagine, the Davis's is very out outgoing, outspoken and competitive.

My dad, better known as "Jimmy D", was self-employed for over 55 years. My dad is today 86 years old and *leading strong*. He instilled a work ethic in each of his children by being an exemplary example each and every day. My brothers are a lot like my father. They are very strong minded, hardworking and family oriented. All the men in my family can be labeled with high self-esteem and as great men.

Now let's focus on those with low self-esteem. I have worked in many different arenas such as work, church and community sectors. I have met numerous people who have had a negative image of themselves and felt bad, ugly, unlikeable or stupid (their word). They either lacked confidence, found it hard to make and keep friendships, and felt victimized by others. They all have common traits. They tend to avoid new things and find change hard. Others can't deal well with personal failure and tend to put themselves down and might say things like "I'm stupid" or "I can't do that". They are not proud of what they achieve and always think they could have done better. Most of them would constantly compare themselves to their peers in a negative way. If you find what was stated above true, then get comfortable, take mental notes, and let's get rid of that weight of low self-esteem.

Think Self-Esteem

The bible makes is very clear, "For as he thinketh in his heart, so is he" Proverbs 23:7, (KJV) The way you think about yourself as a leader is half the battle how you choose to live your life.

Some people seem to have low self-esteem from an early age. This may be partly have their personalities – some people naturally have a more negative outlook on life than others. Or they may have had a challenging experience as a young child, due to health problems, family difficulties or having a parent who was depressed, abusive or neglected them.

Other people develop low self-esteem following a difficult time such as divorce, bereavement or being bullied, and can't bounce back.

Individuals with low self-esteem can find it very hard to cope with life pressures from family, peers and society. They can find it very stressful and feel they are expected to achieve good grades, look a certain way and be successful or popular.

Signs of Low Self-Esteem

How can you lead if you have no self-esteem? Take a moment and look at the symptoms of low self-esteem: The symptoms of low self-esteem can be different depending on who you are.

Can you recognize yourself in any of these low self-esteem signs?

People with low self-esteem:

> Doubtful and do not trust their judgment.
> Fear of rejection and look for approval from others.
> Unassertive in their behavior with others.
> Blame themselves, everything is their fault.
> Seek approval, depends on others to be happy.
> Anxious about the future and are often depressed.
> Not a risk taker, afraid of failure.
> Over compensate and become over-achievers.

- ➤ Perfectionists, and never satisfied.
- ➤ Unable to affirm themselves positively. Are constantly plagued with negative self-talk and self-doubt.
- ➤ Unable to make an honest assessment of their strengths, qualities, and good points; difficult to accept compliments or recognition from others.
- ➤ Insecure, anxious, and nervous when they are with others.
- ➤ Are easily overcome with despair and depression when they experience a setback.
- ➤ Overreact and become de-energized by resentment, anger, and the desire for revenge against those whom they believe have not fully accepted them.
- ➤ Fulfill roles in their family that are counter-productive and co-dependent.
- ➤ Vulnerable to mental health problems.

Acronym – Self-Esteem

S	Remember who you are and take a *"selfie"*.
E	<u>Evaluate</u> your situation.
L	<u>Learn</u> all you can from positive people.
F	*<u>Follow up</u>* on-going for a "better you".
E	*<u>Examine</u>* yourself and then make the necessary adjustments.
S	*<u>Set standards</u>* for your life.
T	*<u>Think</u>* on good things.

E	*Elevate* your mind to accomplish your future goals.
E	*Eliminate* those that are not helping to add value to your life.
M	*Model* people of "good character and integrity".

What can you do to strengthen your self-esteem?

_____

_____

_____

Self-perception

Valuing your self-perception, a specific stage in leading that occurs whenever you are willing to look at your situation objectively. When you do, you will realize that your strengths far outweigh your weaknesses. This exercise can give you the opportunity to validate your positive self-perception of a leader.

1. What three things do I like about myself?

    a.

    b.

    c.

2. What are my strengths?

    a.

    b.

    c.

3. What activities can make me a better and stronger person?

    a.

    b.

    c.

12

Leadership Philosophy

I AM Statement

1. Which of these "I am ..." statements most challenge your current thoughts about who you are?

a.	I am honest.
b.	I am consistent.
c.	I am approachable.

Explain:

2. Do you have mindsets, perspectives or even habits that are rooted in "selfishness" rather than "leadership"?

Explain:_____

_____

_____

3. Which statement(s) is the opposite of leadership?

a. Choosing the right objective.
b. Inspiring others to join you.
c. Choosing the wrong objective (or no objective, that is, just drifting).
d. Applying ineffective or immoral means to achieving your outcome.
e. Disengaging others.

4. Which area of leadership do you need to grow in most? (able to forgive anything and everything, confidence in who you are and what you can accomplish, or confidence about who will follow you).

Explain:_____

_____

_____

_____

_____

Write a Leaders', "I Am Statement" below:

Statement:_____

_____

_____

_____

_____

_____

_____

_____

_____

_____

_____

_____

_____

_____

_____

_____

_____

_____

_____

_____

_____

_____

13

Influence

The two most important conversations that I love having with the youth are regarding influence and authority. The bible says, *"When the righteous thrive, the people rejoice; when the wicked rule, the people groan"*. *Proverbs 29:2 (NIV)*. Godly leadership is very necessary in our lives today.

You can pretty much guess how many organizations will function successfully if the leaders are God-fearing. As youth, it's of most importance for your leaders to lead well, whether it's a boss, principal, coach or a teacher. The bible says, *"Let no one despise you for your youth, but set the believers an example in speech, in conduct, in love, in faith, in purity,"* 1 Timothy 4:12 (ESV).

I can recall as a newlywed, living in a predominately white community. We had no children at the time. It is still so clear to me…. God spoke to me regarding influence. I was sitting on my couch in my country home watching a commercial about baby pampers. I thought as I watched the commercial, when I have children I can't let them go to a predominately white school. That would not be fair to my children to expose them to possible rejections, cruelty, and some prejudiced people.

As soon as that thought came to my mind God spoke to me in that soft voice and said, "Why can't your children be the influences, rather than them being influenced". At that moment, I decided my children would attend school in that community. It was the most pleasant experience for my family. We flourished in that community. Still today we share with others what God's purpose for our lives could detail.

Our youth have so many negative role models that influence them. They have such as troubled friends, family issues, and most of all social media. The bible makes it very clear, *"Do not be deceived: "Bad company ruins good morals." (1 Corinthians 15:33 (ESV).*

Acronym - Influence

I	Leaders have great **Impact** on others.
N	Important tool...**Networking**
F	**Fame** and **Fortune**.
L	**Leverage**
U	**Underestimated**
E	Influence strengthen self- **Esteem**
N	**Notoriety**
C	**Character counts**
E	Spectacular **Effects**

Who has influenced your life the most?

_____

_____

_____

14

Respect

Question: "What does the Bible say about respect?"

Answer: The apostle Peter summarizes the Bible's teaching on respect in his first Epistle: *"Show proper respect to everyone: "Honor everyone. Love the brotherhood. Fear God. Honor the emperor." 1 Peter 2:17(ESV).* This passage encompasses four major areas of our lives. It teaches us that as followers of Christ we should respect all men, other christians, God, and governmental authorities. The word respect means to "honor or value." It literally means "to place a great value or high price on something." (Merriam-Webster.) Interestingly, today we tend to place our values on our personal and selfish needs. However, biblical respect is far different. It is more about a perceived inequality in that we recognize some things and some people are more important. Aretha Franklin said it so well in her song– Respect (Lyrics)- (1990)

> *"You''ve got to show me, got to show me a little….*
> *Yes, all I want is, all I want is a little*
> *What all I need is a little respect…..*
> *And what you need, you know that I''ve got it*
> *All I''m askin'' for is a little respect…..*
> *Respect me, oh I, I-I-I",*
> *Respect (Lyrics)-Aretha Franklin (1990)*

To respect everyone, believers must be conscious that God has created all people in his image, regardless of whether they believe in Christ or not.

We should show them proper respect and honor them because this is the great commandment as stated in the gospel of Mark. Jesus answered, "The most important is, 'Hear, O Israel: The Lord our God, the Lord is one. And you shall love the Lord your God with all your heart and with all your soul and with all your mind and with all your strength.' The second is this: 'You shall love your neighbor as yourself.' There is no other commandment greater than these." And the scribe said to him, "You are right, Teacher. You have truly said that he is one, and there is no other besides him. And to love him with all the heart and with all the understanding and with all the strength, and to love one's neighbor as oneself, is much more than all burnt offerings and sacrifices." And when Jesus saw that he answered wisely, he said to him, "You are not far from the kingdom of God." Mark 12: 29-34 (ESV).

It is very clear in the passages above, God places great emphasis on respectfulness.

Respect is morally important.

It has been several years ago, I was working as a summer school teacher in my school district. I would distribute writing paper and daily assignments to my students. During that procedure I was not concerned with receiving a thank you. Now and then as I would hand back completed class assignments, a few students would show acknowledgement with "Thank you Ms. Kirk." However, it was this young man that would consistently say, "Thank you", when I would give his paper back to him. His gratitude was sincere and warmed my heart as I remember thinking how nice to hear the response because currently that's not the case. Some of our youth today have no discipline, no respect for others and no God in their lives.

One afternoon, at the end of the day, a student came back into the classroom shouting that one of my students was fighting in the parking lot.

I immediately ran out to see what was happening. As I came to the scene, I could see a student sitting in a parked police car with blood dripping from his nose onto his white t-shirt. There were other staff members at the scene as well. What was so disturbing was the young man in the police car was the student that was respectful to me and said "Thank you" all the time. This student started the altercation that turned into a fight. I approached the police car and began to inform the student of my disappointment. As I was engaged in a conversation with this student, the police officer approached me and asked me if I knew this student, and how old this young man was? I told him my relationship to this student. I told the officer that he only had one week left of summer school and could possibly earn a credit that would allow him to be promoted to the next level. Thereafter, the officer asked me if I was willing to take responsibility for him. I said "Yes" and he uncuffed him and released him into my custody.

As I escorted the student home, I shared with him in my opinion what just happened. I began to tell him in no way was the officer supposed to have let him go into my care. I was not related to him. I informed the young man that I believe it was "favor". By this I mean due to him being so respectful to me, God gave him favor. I told him that is why he wasn't arrested. Respect was shown to me and he obtained favor from God.

Acronym - Respect

R	Take **responsibility** for your actions.
E	**Empower** yourself to greatness.
S	**Successful** people respect the process.
P	**Praise** other people.
E	**Exhibit** self-respect.
C	**Consider** everyone's opinions.
T	**Treat** others how you want to be known for...consistently.

How do you show respect?

_____

_____

_____

15

Authority

I facilitated a workshop at my school entitled, "What Does Authority Look Like to You? I can recall on several occasions since then asking that question. The answer is "I don't know". Sad to say, nor do they respond to an authority figure correctly. I had the most respect for all adults when I was young. I have an uncanny respect for authority figures today. No so much for many youths of our society. Face it, "All", authority comes from God. Respect and obeying authority is vital to survival.

Let's examine what the bible says about authority and how to deal with authority in a godly way. *"Submit yourselves for the LORD's sake to every human authority: whether to the emperor, as the supreme authority."* 1 *Peter 2:13. (NIV).*

"Then Jesus came to them and said, "All authority in heaven and on earth has been given to me." Matthew 28:18. (NIV).

Here is a good starting point regarding obeying authority, *"Remind your people to obey the rulers and authorities and not to be rebellious." Titus 3:1. (NIV).*

The only way to not be rebellious is to, "Have confidence in your leaders and submit to their authority, because they keep watch over you as those who must give an account. *Do this so that their work will be a joy, not a burden, for that would be of no benefit to you"*. Hebrews 13: 17, (NIV).

"Let everyone be subject to the governing authorities, for there is no authority except that which God has established." Romans 13:1-7. (NIV).

For a moment, put yourself in these shoes. If you were given the responsibility to lead others to achieve a dream that to them seemed to be unreachable, and unachievable, what would your plan be? As leaders everything we do and every task we face should be approached with that question being at the forefront of your mind.

I believe you must obey authority, it is a life or death matter. You decide, "What does authority look like?" Take a moment and see Jesus. His face, presence and awesome power will no doubt lead you closer to him.

Acronym. - Authority

A	There is **authority** in consistency.
U	We must **understand** others' viewpoints.
T	Don't **tell** someone you are the boss
H	Stay **humble**.
O	**Opt** out when others refused to follow the leader.
R	You have the **right** and power to lead, because of the **respect** you have achieved.
I	**Integrity**
T	**Teamwork**
Y	**You** hold the key.

1. Think of a time when you used your authority to lead others?

_____

_____

16

The Start Of Leadership

Study Guide

Your real leadership experience begins today. I believe a new start for your life is God's way. It's our vision together. I am so excited to be celebrating this decision with you. It is my sincere prayer that you continue to pursue God's purpose for your life.

As you begin your new life as a godly leader in Christ, there are just a few things I recommend getting you started. Please read through the book and, above all, seek to put God first in every area of your life. This one decision will simplify yet change everything.

Congratulations on deciding to be the best leader you can be. Your best days are ahead of you!

17

The Bible Study Method

Things to do as Leaders

L- First *listen* to that still small voice of God and select a bible passage or use a daily devotional, and then choose the verse that particularly spoke to you that day. Be sure to listen for God's answer in your heart. Then pray regarding what you read because it is a two-way conversation.

E-Exalt: Definition – in a state of extreme happiness. This can be as simple as thanking God for helping you use this Scripture.

A- Acknowledge God in everything. Align yourself with God's word and allow him to give you direction each day.

D- Daily devotional. Choose the verse that particularly spoke to your pressing needs that day.

E- End with being thankful for everything. It is the best way to start and finish your day. It keeps everything in perspective. End your devotional time with prayer and thanksgiving.

R- Read and meditate on the verse(s) and allow God to speak to you throughout the day. Highlight, underline or bookmark the scriptures that stand out. What do you think God is saying to you in this verse? Ask

God to teach you and reveal his truth to you. In your own words write this scripture in your journal and personalize what you've read. Perhaps it's instruction, encouragement, a new promise, or correction for a area of your life. Write down how this scripture applies to you today.

S- Say It. Speak the word of God out loud. *"Study to show thyself approved unto God, a workman that needeth not to be ashamed, rightly dividing the word of truth". 2 Timothy 2:15(KJV)*

Three Truths Leaders Need to Remember

1. *You are the righteousness of God in Christ.*

"Therefore, since we have been made right in God's sight by faith, we have peace with God because of what Jesus Christ our Lord has done for us." Romans 5:2(NLT)

2. *You are a new creature.*

"This means anyone who belongs to Christ has become a new person. The old life is gone; a new life has begun!" 2 Corinthians 5:17(NLT)

3. *You are becoming more and more like Jesus.*

"So all of us who have had that veil removed can see and reflect the glory of the Lord. And the Lord – who is Spirit – makes us more and more like him as we are changed into his glorious image." 2 Corinthians 3:18(NLT)

Therefore, act like it. Live like it. And above all, confess it!

A Leaders Life

"When the righteous are in authority, the people rejoice: but when the wicked beareth rule, the people mourn." Proverbs 29:2. (KJV)

Leaders are: Not Prideful. Not Self-seeking.

A lot of youth think they aren't cut out for leadership. But if you love Jesus and you care about others and the things of God, everything else falls into place.

In my eleven years working with school students, I've met multiple students who are and could be incredible leaders. It's not for their spunky personalities and out of the box thinking. They have a passion for people. When you boil it down, that's what really matters.

If you start with Jesus every day, all the intricacies of leading should align conceptually, biblically, and practically. You should be able to trace everything back to Jesus.

Guide to Staying Interested...

- Find something you are passionate about, whether it is a sport or a musical instrument. This is a great way to help build a good attitude. "You take the opportunity to make some goals and objectives. If you feel like you are getting something accomplished, it makes a difference in your life.

- Set goals for yourself personally and academically. "Kids today don't go to a class called goal setting, "So others don't know what your dreams are, and they don't know what you are trying to accomplish."

- Set objectives to help you set long-term goals and follow through on daily objectives. This is how you get on the road to success.

- Get organized once goals and objectives are set, you want to see outcomes. Writing down a to-do list on a large wall calendar can help you stay on top of those goals.

- Make a commitment following through on daily tasks is so important. The task can be anything.

- Find someone that you are inspired by. One thing that really inspires is stories. Telling stories about powerful things that other people are doing is one way that you can keep motivated and motivate other people.

18

Ten things a youth leader needs:

1. A Purpose for Everything.

Let's be honest. From my perspective there is a lot of weird stuff that happens amongst the youth. Sleep over all night skating parties, and an endless list of games, and programs that don't seem in any way connected to sharing the gospel.

But if you know the purpose behind each component, then even the goofy and weird parts make sense.

A realistic leader interacting with the youth can create laughter, break down walls, and show kids that there is a childlike joy in everyone. For leaders those same activities can offer an opportunity to step out of their own comfort zone and put kids before themselves.

Do you know your purpose? If so, what is it?

Note:

_____

_____

_____

2. Remain teachable.

I was a kid once. If you're made of flesh and blood, you probably made a few choices that you aren't proud of. It is not always best to share all the details of your life without a relational foundation. But the more vulnerable you are with others, the more likely they are to share their short comings with you. If we hide, so do they. Be honest and learn from your mistakes and others.

What teachable moment(s) can you remember?

Note:

_____

_____

_____

3. Seek out others that need help.

No matter how awesome a leader you are, there will always be kids in the corner that are hoping to be seen or not. They show up for all reasons. Because their parents made them, or a friend invited them. Either way God has brought them into your path, and he's entrusted them to you for help.

Who have you noticed standing in a corner to see if anyone will notice them?

Note:

_____

_____

_____

4. Be able to share the good and bad experiences.

Sometimes life can be "so hard". A lot of kids think it is because they are only exposed to things that have no substance or purpose in their life.

What they choose to do has no lasting truth. Nor is it applicable to their lives today.

What good or bad experiences have you faced?

Note:

_____

_____

_____

5. Know your audience:

Knowing others means more than just knowing who they are. It means knowing how they will respond to different situations and preparing likewise with them in mind.

Some people love being the center of attention, and some people fall apart when you put them in a different role. It's important to give everyone an equal opportunity to shine. However, the risk of humiliating anyone or making a person feel alone and outcast is not worth the potential reward of making them feel adored.

When you are exposed to a person for the first time and you've never had any interaction with them, you might want to be careful about throwing them into a situation that requires them to be outgoing and comfortable in front of everyone.

It's also important to know where people are spiritually. This doesn't mean you should ask every kid who comes through the door, "Do you believe in Jesus?" Those conversations should happen, but not before you develop a relationship with them (know your audience) and earn the right to ask those deeply intimate questions.

Over-spiritualizing a person's experience can prevent them from having a spiritual experience." Youth leadership is an excellent context to practice reflecting Christ through the way you love and live.

Can you discern where people are spiritually?

Note:

_____

_____

_____

6. Don't embarrass kids

Our youth can live in constant fear of humiliation. The last thing you would want to happen is that they should have to live out their worst nightmares exposed to ridicule. They need to learn that they are valued and accepted by others.

If you know someone well enough and you're confident that their spirit will allow them to embrace and appreciate the experience, and the embarrassment serves a purpose, mild embarrassment may be acceptable.

Can you think of a time when you were embarrassed by someone?

Note:

_____

_____

_____

7. Build Relationship with Families

You could be the nicest, most caring and trustworthy person on the planet. But if parents don't know you, how can you expect them to trust you with their loved one?

Building a relationship with family members is especially important for middle school and elementary school ministries. Where kids are fully dependent on their parents to even be able to show up at events. Sometimes meeting parents is effortless because they actively seek out the leaders who work with their kids. Other times, meeting parents takes work.

Are you comfortable interacting with adults?

Note:

_____

_____

_____

8.Put your relationship with Jesus first.

But seek ye first the kingdom of God, and his righteousness; and all these things shall be added unto you. Matthew 6:33. KJV

This may seem selfish in a way. The reality is the more we put Jesus first, the more we love those around us. When you put your relationship with Jesus first the purpose and significance of everything you do and say to others is amplified, not reduced.

Phrases like, "You can only lead someone as far as you've gone" may be cliché, but they still carry weight. If you aren't pursuing your own relationship with Jesus, how can you honestly encourage others that it's important to their faith? If you aren't reading your bible, praying, and surrounding yourself with christians who are wiser than yourself, you aren't offering your best.

What are your tools of the trade and what resources can you use to lead others?

Note:

_____

_____

_____

9. Honor your commitment

Stepping into leadership roles of any kind is something that should be prayerfully considered, discussed with God and with wise people in your life, and surrounded with spiritual preparation.

If you've committed to leading others at your school, church or through another organization, honor God, others, and the leaders on your team by being trustworthy, accountable, and invested in the work you are doing together.

Today's kids have been dubbed "the fatherless generation." Youth leaders can't abandon them too. Leaving ministry should be considered just as carefully and prayerfully as entering it.

As a leader what commitments are you willing to make in leading others?

Note:

_____

_____

_____

10. Get a Mentor

One of the biggest dangers facing people in ministry is the, "I know it all mentality". It's easy to be excited about something when you first get going. After a couple of years how do you stay excited? And more importantly, how do you draw from your experience while still treating each experience and each other as something entirely new and wonderful? The key is having a mentor. A mentor is someone that constantly is pouring into the life of the mentee. If nobody is pouring into you, sooner or later you're going to feel empty. Whether that mentor is a pastor, a more experienced leader, or a wise friend, you need someone who can offer you fresh perspective, hold you accountable, pray for you, love you, and inspire you to keep going, *"And let us consider how we may spur one another on toward love and good deeds," Hebrews 10:24.(NIV)*

What do you think the role of a mentor should be today?

Note:

_____

_____

_____

A Confident Leader should know:

Be confident that God forgives anything and everything.

"If we confess our sins, he is faithful and just and will forgive us our sins and purify us from all unrighteousness." 1 John 1:9 (NIV)

He will forgive you when you ask. And as you keep walking with God, he will give you the strength to keep getting up and moving forward.

"…for though the righteous fall seven times, they rise again, but the wicked stumble when calamity strikes." Proverbs 24:16 (NIV)

Be confident in who God is and what he's done for you.

Know that God is our Heavenly Father.

He loves us and cares for us and wants the best for us. The thing that we need to keep in mind is that we are his children and he will never disown us or leave us.

There is nothing more that we can do to earn God's approval. The biggest part of being confident is being confident in his word.

List below what you could do to help build your confidence?

Note:

_____

_____

_____

_____

_____

_____

_____

_____

Carolyn J. Kirk

Explain: Key Word in the verse.

THE BIBLE SAYS:

☐ ... "I am the light of the world." //John 8:12 (ESV)

LIGHT:_____

_____

☐ I am "made the righteousness of God in Him". // 2 Corinthians 5:21(KJV)

RIGHTEOUSNESS:_____

_____

☐ I am.. "holy and without blame before him in love:" // Ephesians 1:4(KJV)

HOLY:_____

_____

☐ I am... "because of his great love for us // Ephesians 2:4(NIV)

LOVE:_____

_____

☐ I am... "alive with Christ even when we were dead in transgressions-"// Ephesians 2:5(NIV)

ALIVE:_____

_____

☐ I am "created in Christ Jesus to do good works," // Ephesians 2:10 (NIV)

CREATED:_____

_____

☐ "I am not saying this because I am in need, for I have learned to be content whatever the circumstances." // Philippians 4:11(IV)

CONTENT:_____

_____

☐ "I can do all this through him who gives me strength" // Philippians 4:13(NIV)

CAN:_____

_____

☐ I am "being strengthened with all power according to his glorious might so that you may have great endurance and patience" // Colossians 1:11(NIV)

ENDURANCE:_____

_____

☐ I am "in whom are hidden all the treasures of wisdom and knowledge". // Colossians 2:3 (NIV)

WISDOM:_____

_____

I Am Study Questions

1. Which of the previous "I am…" statements most challenge your current thoughts about who you are?

2. Do you have mindsets, perspectives or even habits that are rooted in "religion" rather than "relationship"?

3. Which area of spiritual confidence do you need to grow in most?

(Confidence that God forgives anything and everything, confidence in who God is and what he's done for you, or confidence about who you are in Christ?

Write, " A Statement of Faith " statement:

_____
_____
_____
_____
_____
_____
_____
_____
_____
_____
_____
_____
_____
_____
_____
_____
_____

20

Living A Changed Life as A Leader

Now that you've had this amazing experience of accepting responsibility as a leader, receiving instruction, and making a change as a new believer, it is all about living the kind of life God wants you to live.

As a new leader You need to remember...

1. The life we live for God is a process. Even though you are now "saved" and full of the presence of God, you will now need God's help to transform your life.

The Bible teaches us that we are one person, but we have different aspects of our being.

"May God himself, the God of peace, sanctify you through and through. May your whole spirit, soul, and body be kept blameless at the coming of our Lord Jesus Christ. 1 Thessalonians 5:23 (NIV)

2. We have a spirit, a soul, and a body.

Our spirit refers to that part of our being where the presence of God resides. Our soul is made up of our mind, our emotions, and our will. How we think (our mind), how we feel (our emotions), and the choices we make (our will). Our body is the house that we were born into.

3. When we make a new beginning the bible teaches us that we are born again. "In reply Jesus declared, 'I tell you the truth, no one can see the kingdom of God unless he is born again." John 3:3 (NIV)

When you accepted Jesus, a new you was born. The problem is the old you, the sinful nature, remains and these two are in conflict.

4. There will be conflict. (Natural vs Spiritual.)

"For the sinful nature desires what is contrary to the spirit, and the spirit what is contrary to the sinful nature." Galatians 5:17 (NIV).

5. There will be struggles.

Apostle Paul who was an amazing Christian, great theologian, and wrote the majority of the New Testament. He struggled with this conflict and wrote about it in the book of Romans 7:18-23. (NIV)

☐ We all have the desire to do good. (v.18)

☐ I need to be willing to do the will of God. (v. 19-20)

☐ Guard my mind. (v. 21-23)

The Apostle Paul referred to this struggle as "the good fight of faith" because even though it is a struggle it is worth it!

6. The part God wants to change is our soul.

"May God himself, the God of peace, sanctify you through and through. May your whole spirit, soul and body be kept blameless at the coming of the Lord Jesus Christ." 1 Thessalonians 5:23 (NIV)

☐ It is God himself who changes us.

☐ He is the God of peace.

☐ God is thorough.

What season(s) are you in regarding leadership?

Sometimes we can allow the opinions and thoughts of others to hinder us regarding how we live and think. Before you decide where you are regarding the seasons of life? Here's a thought! Are you in summer mode and wearing a hat and gloves? Is it winter and you're in a bikini? This might sound strange to you. However, we often try to cover up our problems with the wrong coverings. It is so important that we surround ourselves with people that can help us. It is also equally important to watch what we say. The bible says, *"Don't use foul or abusive language. Let everything you say be good and helpful, so that your words will be an encouragement to those who hear them."* *Ephesians 4:29 (NLT)*

It is very difficult to guard against the elements and respond accordingly. You must first empty your mind of all the false beliefs you've been taught (including the poor ideas and thoughts).

Let's determine where you are today regarding weathering the storms in your life.

What season are you in? If you want to discover your true season(s) in life, complete this exercise below.

Give it a shot! At the very least, you'll learn one of two things: your true season in life -or- that you should really think about your life.

Here's what to do:

1. Below circle the season(s).

Spring	Summer	Winter	Fall

2. Why do you feel that way.

_____

_____

_____

_____

3. Do you like the season(s) you are in? If not, write any answer(s) that pops into your head that will help you change seasons. It doesn't have to be a complete sentence. A short phrase is fine.

_____

_____

_____

_____

_____

_____

_____

_____

Nest Steps:

Write a plan for your desired season.

_____

_____

_____

_____

_____

_____

_____

Last step is to share the plan with someone you trust.

21

Instructions for Godly Leadership

Be godly (holy)...

It is very important to live a life that is pleasing to God. We see many hypocritical people representing christianity. Therefore, placing a poor perspective on the people of God. The bible clearly tells us to be holy. How can we lead effectively if our character and integrity is questionable as leaders?

"because it is written, "YOU SHALL BE HOLY, FOR I AM HOLY."
1 Peter 1:16 (NASB)

Pay attention to instructions...

People will pay attention and listen if we communicate clearly our explanations. When instructions are given and it is not clear or defined what the leader expects, the desired outcomes are not realized. Also the task is not complete and people are left frustrated. Not only the fact that things aren't done, but the leader has failed.

"Pay attention, my people, to my instruction! Listen to the words I speak! I will sing a song that imparts wisdom; I will make insightful observations about the past. What we have heard and learned—that which our ancestors have told us. We will not hide from their descendants. We will tell the next generation about the Lord's praiseworthy acts, about his strength and the amazing things he has done. Psalms 78:1-4. (NET)

Demonstrate God's love for his people...

The very nature of God himself is love. The bible teaches that, "God is love." Not only does God love; love is part of his essential nature. Love is who God is. Therefore he cannot but love. Genuine love has no color, no face, no gender, and no conditions.

Anyone who does not love does not know God, because God is love. 1 John 4:8(ESV)

Write it down...

I have observed my daughters over the years write down things they wanted to achieve. Today both have been blessed to see those desires unfold before their very eyes. Again, the bible instructs us to write down our visions and run with it. Believing that God is a promise keeper. But we must do our part in obedience and ask, believing his word.

"And the LORD answered me: "Write the vision; make it plain on tablets, so he may run who reads it." Habakkuk 2:2(ESV).

22

Journaling...

My Journey to A Godly Leader!

Steps to Journaling:

L-listen

    E-experience

        A-accuracy

           D-dialog

                E-educate

                    R-review

                        S- short

Journal Notes:

What type of leadership styles do you want?

_____

_____

What kind of leader do you want to be?

_____

_____

What will your approach to leadership be?

_____

_____

Carolyn J. Kirk

I OBSERVED A LEADER TODAY DO THIS....
What I learned...
(Good or Bad)

Notes:

_____

_____

_____

_____

_____

_____

_____

_____

_____

_____

_____

_____

_____

_____

_____

_____

_____

_____

_____

_____

_____

Notes:

_____

_____

_____

_____

_____

_____

_____

_____

_____

_____

_____

_____

_____

_____

_____

_____

_____

_____

_____

_____

_____

_____

_____

_____

_____

_____

Carolyn J. Kirk

Notes:

Keep A Good Perspective

As you look for good leadership examples, don't be discourage by what you see. Remove all temptations and distractions from your mind. Use every opportunity to learn from all leaders, whether good or bad, when working to improve your leadership skills. Use those examples to determine your leadership style and approach. But remember your attitude is the key to your success and the purpose of keeping a good perspective. If you make this a habit, you will control your ability to be positive and create a foundation for achieving your goals. We were created with the "mind of Christ". Ask yourself, "Is this how God thinks?"

Ephesians 4:23 – "...be made new in the attitude of your minds." (NIV)

If you're not happy with what you see, look at what you are putting in your heart.

The most powerful tool in renewing our minds and breaking free from negative thinking patterns is God's word.

"For as he thinketh in his heart, so is he: Eat and drink, saith he to thee; but his heart is not with thee." Proverbs 23:7 (KJV)

God's word teaches us that...

Godly leaders exist:

1. To teach us.

2. To encourage us.

3. To give us advice.

"Obey your leaders and submit to their authority. They keep watch over you as men who must give an account. Obey them so that their work will be a joy, not a burden, for that would be of no advantage to you." Hebrews 13:17 (AMP)

"Submit to one another out of reverence for Christ." Ephesians 5:21(NIV)

Godly leaders have a voice:

The Bible teaches us that Jesus is our shepherd and we are his sheep. He is constantly speaking to us and leading us.

"When he has brought out all his own, he goes on ahead of them, and his sheep follow him because they know his voice." John 10:4 (NIV)

God speaks to us by the Holy Spirit in our heart. God's voice will never contradict his word.

What is God saying to you?

Note:

_____

_____

_____

Spiritual Freedom

To grow spiritually, we need to be free.

Spiritual freedom brings spiritual maturity. Spiritual freedom comes as we allow God to change and transform our lives through his word, his people and his voice.

"...being confident of this, that he who began a good work in you will carry it on to completion until the day of Christ Jesus." Philippians 1:6 (NIV)

What weights are holding you down from being free?

Note:_____

_____

_____

_____

As we look close at this experience below are questions for your consideration.

Leadership is not prescriptive and what works for one person may not work for another. There is one trait, however, that many successful leaders share. They are constantly asking themselves questions to stay relevant and perceptive.

Keeping tabs on your own leadership development might help figure out areas for improvement, deepen your understanding of your purpose and passion and set a good example to the people you lead.

As you take this journey to remove the **lead** from **leadership** before your **ship** sinks..., ask yourself these eight questions to help you grow as an individual and as a leader:

1. What did I achieve?

_____

_____

_____

_____

2. What mistakes did I make and how can I learn from them?

_____

_____

_____

_____

3. Did I help someone else succeed today?

_____

_____

_____

_____

4.What motivated me?

_____

_____

_____

_____

5. Did I work toward my goals?

_____

_____

_____

_____

6. What stumbling blocks did I come across?

_____

_____

_____

_____

7. What do I need to release or let go of?

_____

_____

_____

_____

8. What legacy do I want to leave behind?

_____

_____

_____

_____

23

Mission Possible

A vision and mission statement can be the anchor points of any good leader's success plan. This exercise will take you through the process of writing a mission and vision statement, with goals and objectives to help guide you along the way.

Why is it so important to write down your goals and objectives in the form of a mission and vision statement?

"And the LORD answered me: "Write the vision; make it plain on tablets, so he may run who reads it." Habakkuk 2:2 (ESV)

Definition: Mission Statement

A mission statement is a statement of the purpose of a company, organization or person; its reason for existing; a written declaration of an organization's core purpose and focus that normally remains unchanged over time. Wikipedia

A mission statement talks about how you will get to your desired end.

Write a Personal Leaders Mission Statement:

_____

_____

_____

_____

_____

_____

_____

_____

_____

_____

_____

_____

Definition: Vision Statement

A vision statement is a declaration of an organization's objectives, intended to guide its internal decision-making. A vision statement is not limited to business organizations and may also be used by non-profit or governmental entities.

The ability to think about or plan the future with imagination or wisdom. Merriam-Webster

A vision statement outlines where you want to be in your future goals.

Write a Personal Leaders Vision Statement:

_____

_____

_____

_____

_____

_____

_____

_____

Definition: Goals Statement:

A goal statement is a text intended to provide insight into the personal, career and educational goals of an applicant. The statement demonstrates the writing skills of the applicant and gives a glimpse of his personality. Merriam-Webster

A goals statement outlines those future goals you want to achieve.

Write a Personal Leaders Goals Statement:

_____

_____

_____

_____

_____

_____

_____

_____

Definition: Objective Statement – An objective statement in the business context, is comprised of a sentence or two that describes the exact outcomes that the business wants. It tells employees precisely what they must do to reach the company's goals. Wikipedia

An objective statement outlines the deadlines. They are realistic, are specific and are achievable.

Write a Personal Leaders Objectives Statement:

_____

_____

_____

_____

_____

_____

_____

_____

Types of Leadership Styles

I have worked in several professions during my 35 years of experience. (Based on my experience.) I have learned quickly the difference between a" good and bad" leader. Regardless of his or her ability as leaders, one can benefit by both.

Below are my examples of 4 different leadership styles.

"Earn yo.ur leadership every day." --Michael Jordan

Definition: Leadership style

A leadership style is a leader's style of providing direction, implementing plans, and motivating people. There are many different leadership styles that can be exhibited by leaders in the political, business or other fields. Wikipedia

4 Different Types of Leadership Styles

1. _Appreciative Leadership Style_- Expressing heart-felt appreciation and positive encouragement. Sometimes being "nice" goes a long way in time of challenging tasks and dealing with difficult people.
2. _"Bossy Betty" Leadership Style_- Dominant leaders cast the vision. However, this type of leader can hinder team involvement. This leadership style can work quite well if you are liked and admired.

(Deb S). Sometimes this leadership style can help drive a person to the top. But, can you stay there?

3. *"Delegative" Leadership Style*- I believe a leader that can effectively delegate shows strong leadership skills. Not all leaders can delegate. This is due to the fact the leader has not been a good example, or not trusted by his or her followers. A good delegator can get everybody aligned and moving toward the same vision.

4. *"Got My Back "Leadership Style*- This style of leadership does not demonstrate confidence or a strong vision and instead he or she wants employees to come up with innovative and creative strategies to help them lead successfully.

Activity:

Interview a leader, a pastor, teacher or a boss. Shadow that individual and journal that experience.

I interviewed:

_____

_____

_____

_____

_____

_____

_____

_____

_____

_____

_____

_____

What style of leader are you?

_____

_____

_____

_____

_____

_____

_____

_____

_____

_____

What type of leader do you want to become?

_____

_____

_____

_____

_____

_____

_____

_____

_____

_____

24

Personal examples that helped shape my Leadership Styles

What do you have in your hands that you can use to be blessed by and be a blessing to others?

Elisha Multiplies the Widow's Oil

"Elisha said to her, "What shall I do for you? Tell me, what do you have in the house?" And she said, "Your maidservant has nothing in the house except a jar of oil." Then he said, "Go, borrow vessels at large for yourself from all your neighbors, even empty vessels; do not get a few. "And you shall go in and shut the door behind you and your sons, and pour out into all these vessels, and you shall set aside what is full."...2 King 2: 4 (NASB). The widow only had a jar of oil. God can use and multiple what you naturally possess (God given gifts and talents).

Seven categories that helped shape my leadership style.

A Large Family:

My parents have thirteen children, four boys and nine girls. We have two sets of twins in our family. I have a twin brother (Jimmy). Can you imagine having thirteen kids and each one different than the next? I can recall having a conversation with my mother about very serious and confidential matters. I knew that other family members would have similar concerns. My mother could hold conversations with all of us and never share what the others would tell her. This woman was amazing. My mother could keep a secret. **What I have learned that helped shape my leadership style in this category is confidentiality, sharing, looking out for others, organization, don't gossip and respect others property.**

"Tomboy" Life Style:

I grew up as a "Tomboy". Definition of a tomboy is a girl who exhibits characteristics or behaviors considered typical of a boy, including wearing masculine clothing and engaging in games and activities that are physical in nature... Wikipedia

I could be seen daily in the neighborhood park, wearing jogging pants, high top tennis shoes or overalls. I love sports. Every day and all day, I would be at the park playing basketball, or tennis with only the boys.

The school district I attend did not have a girls' basketball team during my high school years. Still today, I love the sport, but I do not watch girls play because it does not hold my interest. **What I have learned that helped shape my leadership style in this category is to be a team player. I can pick team members by his or her skill sets. I also have learned how to "work and play" with the opposite sex. Every leadership position I've held, I have been the only African American woman and the organizations were predominately men that held leadership roles.**

My Junior High School Teacher:

I cannot say enough about my music teacher Ms. Joy Peters (now in heaven). This woman was the epidemy of an example of an outstanding educator. Over the years, she became my best friend. Ms. Peters accepted me regardless of my skin color and my teenage school behavior. She was a good mentor. Ms. Peters provide financial support to me while I was in college. **What I have learned that helped shape my leadership style in this category is acceptance. Ms. Peters, by her accepting of me helped me to accept people's differences and races and not be judgmental.**

My First Job:

I had the opportunity to interview for a Fortune 500 company in which I was hired before graduating from college. It was my first real interview or, better yet my first real job opportunity. A friend of mine asked me to assist her during a scheduled interview. I was a walk-in. I was hired on the spot to fill one opening the company had even though I was not pursuing a job. The employer stated that I was either very confident or I was faking it until I made it. Those were not his exact words; I cleaned them up a bit.

What I have learned that helped shape my leadership style in this category is confidence, creativity, quick thinker, how to listen, problem solving and to communicate effectively.

Church Experience:

I was sitting in the congregation at my local church listening to my Senior Pastor. As I was totally engaged in the message, all of a sudden, a still small voice spoke to me, "YOU CAN TRUST HIM". After, more than thirty-five years I am still an active member in this ministry. **What I have learned that helped shape my leadership style in this category is character, integrity and trust.**

Marriage:

I was married for fourteen years before I divorced. I had taken a vow to become one; however, we remained two different individuals by choice. I didn't want my kids to become a statistic because of my ex-husband

and my decision to separate. I prayed and asked God to shield them from the stereotypes of divorced children. Praise God! I can say today my daughters are very confident, secure, and balanced young Christian women. **What I have learned that helped shape my leadership style in this category is that I can go through a traumatic experience and come out stronger. Initially it was a challenge to be an example to my children. Nevertheless, I showed them it was possible to go through a divorce and not let that change who God says I am.**

Education:

I was the first one in my family to get a four-year college degree and later my master's degree. I graduated from college in three years. I really did not care for the college lifestyle. I knew I wanted a college degree. Therefore, I did not plan to make it a lifelong career choice, so I got in and out in a hurry. **What I have learned that helped shape my leadership style in this category is that an education affords you power and authority.**

"Leaders aren't born, they are made. And they are made just like anything else, through hard work. And that's the price we'll have to pay to achieve that goal, or any goal."--Vince Lombardi

25

The God Mode

Enable God... to move in your life!

We can learn all the skills and attributes that are necessary to become great leaders. However, if we fail to include God in our daily affairs we will surely perish as leaders. Utilize the God mode listed below as a guide to help you to "enable" God to move in your life and ensure your success in society today. The bible says, *"And God is able to bless you abundantly, so that in all things at all times, having all that you need, you will abound in every good work"*, *2 Corinthians 9:8 (NIV)*. God has provided us with everything we need. However, if we don't give God access into our life to take control, we will never realize his purpose.

<u>Definition of Enable</u>: to give (someone or something) the authority or means to do something:

The God Mode:

E	Earnest prayer

"Rejoice always, pray without ceasing, give thanks in all circumstances; for this is the will of God in Christ Jesus for you". 1 Thessalonians 5:16-18 (ESV)

"Confess your faults one to another, and pray one for another, that ye may be healed. The effectual fervent prayer of a righteous man availeth much". James 5:16 (KJV)

"Be anxious for nothing, but in everything by prayer and supplication, with thanksgiving, let your requests be made known to God; and the peace of God, which surpasses all understanding, will guard your hearts and minds through Christ Jesus." Philippians 4:6-7 NKJV

N	Never doubt

But Jesus looked at them and said to them, "With men this is impossible, but with God all things are possible." Matthew 19:23-26 (NKJV)

"Then he [Jesus] said to Thomas, "Put your finger here; see my hands. Reach out your hand and put it into my side. Stop doubting and believe." John 20:27 (NIV)

"Jesus immediately reached out his hand and took hold of him, saying to him, "O you of little faith, why did you doubt?" Matthew 14:31 (ESV)

"But let him ask in faith, with no doubting, for the one who doubts is like a wave of the sea that is driven and tossed by the wind." James 1:6 (ESV)

"And when they saw him they worshiped him, but some doubted." Matthew 28:17 (ESV)

"Truly, I say to you, whoever says to this mountain, 'Be taken up and thrown into the sea,' and does not doubt in his heart, but believes that what he says will come to pass, it will be done for him". Mark 11:23 (ESV)

"Jesus replied, "Truly I tell you, if you have faith and do not doubt, not only can you do what was done to the fig tree, but also you can say to this mountain, 'Go, throw yourself into the sea,' and it will be done." Matthew 21:21 (NKJV)

"I desire therefore that the men pray everywhere, lifting up holy hands, without wrath and doubting;" 1 Timothy 2:8 (NKJV)

A	Ask

"Ask, and it shall be given you; seek, and ye shall find; knock, and it shall be opened unto you: For every one that asketh receiveth; and he that seeketh findeth; and to him that knocketh it shall be opened." Matthew 7:7-8 (KJV).

"In that day you will no longer ask me anything. Very truly I tell you, my Father will give you whatever you ask in my name. Until now you have not asked for anything in my name. Ask and you will receive, and your joy will be complete." John 16:23-24

"When you ask, you do not receive, because you ask with wrong motives, that you may spend what you get on your pleasures." James 4:3

"Ask, and it will be given to you; seek, and you will find; knock, and it will be opened to you. For everyone who asks receives, and the one who seeks finds, and to the one who knocks it will be opened". Matthew 7:7-8 ESV

B	Boundaries

"See, I have set the land before you. Go in and take possession of the land that the Lord swore to your fathers, to Abraham, to Isaac, and to Jacob, to give to them and to their offspring after them." Deuteronomy 1:8 ESV

"Finally, brothers, whatever is true, whatever is honorable, whatever is just, whatever is pure, whatever is lovely, whatever is commendable, if there is any excellence, if there is anything worthy of praise, think about these things." Philippians 4:8 ESV

"Little by little I will drive them out from before you, until you have increased and possess the land. And I will set your border from the Red Sea to the Sea of the Philistines, and from the wilderness to the Euphrates, for I will give the inhabitants of the land into your hand, and you shall drive them out before you." Exodus 23:30-31 ESV

"Thus says the Lord God: "This is the boundary by which you shall divide the land for inheritance among the twelve tribes of Israel. Joseph shall have two portions. And you shall divide equally what I swore to give to your fathers. This land shall fall to you as your inheritance. "This shall be the boundary of the land: On the north side, from the Great Sea by way of Hethlon to Lebo-hamath, and on to Zedad, Berothah, Sibraim (which lies on the border between Damascus and Hamath), as far as Hazer-hatticon, which is on the border of Hauran. So the boundary shall run from the sea to Hazar-enan, which is on the northern border of Damascus, with the border of Hamath to the north. This shall be the north side. ..." Ezekiel 47:13-23 ESV

L	Listen

"Do not merely listen to the word, and so deceive yourselves. Do what it says". James 1:22 22

"Every good and perfect gift is from above, coming down from the Father of the heavenly lights, who does not change like shifting shadows. He chose to give us birth through the word of truth, that we might be a kind of firstfruits of all he created. My dear brothers and sisters, take note of this:

Everyone should be quick to listen, slow to speak and slow to become angry, because human anger does not produce the righteousness that God desires. Therefore, get rid of all moral filth and the evil that is so prevalent and humbly accept the word planted in you, which can save you. Do not merely listen to the word, and so deceive yourselves. Do what it says. Anyone who listens to the word but does not do what it says is like someone who looks at his face in a mirror and, after looking at himself, goes away and immediately forgets what he looks like. But whoever looks intently into the perfect law that gives freedom and continues in it-not forgetting what they have heard but doing it-they will be blessed in what they do". James 1:17-25

E	Early

"I love those who love me, and those who seek me find me." Proverbs 8:17

"Seek ye the LORD while he may be found, call ye upon him while he is near:" Isaiah 55: 6-7. KJV

"In the morning, LORD, you hear my voice; in the morning I lay my requests before you and wait expectantly." Psalm 5:3

"Let the morning bring me word of your unfailing love, for I have put my trust in you. Show me the way I should go, for to you I entrust my life." Psalm 143:8 KJV

"Because of the LORD's great love we are not consumed, for his compassions never fail. They are new every morning; great is your faithfulness. "Lamentations 3:22-23 KJV

"For His anger is but for a moment, His favor is for a lifetime; Weeping may last for the night, But a shout of joy comes in the morning." Hosea 6:4 KJV

Prayer:

Dear Lord Jesus,

My purpose is to seek you early. Your word instructed us to seek you early while you may be found. Lord you said to pray without ceasing and to give thanks in all circumstances; for this is the will of God in Christ Jesus...

Today, I enable the GOD MODE in my life and cast my entire burden on you Lord. Thank you for sustaining me and never permitting me as your child to be moved or distracted by the temporary problems that I face. I give you permission to take total control.

I want to thank you, for your faithfulness to me and my family and love ones. Your word says to never doubt but believe in our hearts... because you can do anything but fail.

Lord, I come to you asking, and believing I have received all in which I have need of, and that it is mine in Jesus name. I am praying within the boundaries and promises of your word. I am yielding to enable you to take full control of my life. I want your perfect will to be done in me.

I will not just listen to the word of God but I will do what it says. Lord I submit my will to your perfect will.

Thank you, Lord, for your goodness, mercy and your grace!

Lord, I know you love me, and I love you.

Thank you! Thank you!

In Jesus Name Amen!

26

The Journey Starts!!!!!

Here's the challenge. **Stay Afloat! The Start of Leadership** begins with you. I pray that everyone is successful in their endeavors to become a great leader. However, use your **leadership skills to lead all the way through from A to Z.** Stay in the boat if you can't float yet, **there's safety in the boat. Instructions for Godly leadership:** Remember to **cast all your weights (negativity) overboard** to alleviate the load and **keep a good perspective.** Hopefully, **"The Leaders / Leadership Surveys"**, has helped you to identify your strength and build up your **self-esteem, confidence, and level of influence. Respect** the process and listen to those who are **authority** figures in your life. Remember, stay the course. No matter how high you get...**Keep Your Feet Anchored** to the ground.

Smooth Sailing!

About the Author

Carolyn J. Kirk earned her master's degree in Administration Education at Eastern Illinois University in Charleston, Illinois and her bachelor's degree in Industrial Technology & Occupational Safety at Illinois State University in Normal, Illinois. Carolyn is a consultant and motivational speaker for Leadership 4 Advancement Training Center in Danville Illinois, which she founded in 1999. Leadership 4 Advancement Training Center provides training in leadership development for businesses/corporations, educational institutions, and community organizations.

Carolyn also develops and customizes her training workshops for faith-based organizations by providing empowerment initiatives that will enhance her clients' skills in preparing and teaching the Word.

Carolyn J. Kirk has over 30 years of leadership development and training, with an emphasis on Godly, personal and professional development. Her experience includes team training and development, staff development, leadership training, youth educational programs, production management, and occupational safety training for supervisors.

Carolyn is actively involved in churches, schools and health initiatives in her community. She is the president of Women in Leadership Ministries, and she is the founder of Godly Singles Connections Ministries. Carolyn has been a member of her local church for 35 years, which she has served in many capacities. Carolyn is currently employed by Danville School District #118 as the Hearing Officer. Carolyn reports disciplinary actions taken against the school children to the District's Board of Education.

Carolyn resides in Danville, Illinois. She has two daughters, Erica and Carly Kirk.

Printed in the United States
By Bookmasters